AMERICAN CLASSIC

Car Poems *for* Collectors

AMERICAN CLASSIC

Car Poems *for* Collectors

Edited by Mary Swope & Walter H. Kerr
Introduction: Reed Whittemore

SCOP EIGHT
SCOP Publications, Inc.
College Park, Maryland

AMERICAN CLASSIC: Car Poems for Collectors
Copyright © 1985 by SCOP Publications, Inc.
Editors: Mary Swope & Walter H. Kerr

Made possible in part by contributions from Friends of SCOP and International Union, United Automobile, Aerospace & Agricultural Implement Workers of America (UAW).

EDITORS' NOTE: Three of these poems appeared in *The Michigan Quarterly Review*, Vol. XIX No. 4,/Vol. XX No. 1 "The Automobile and American Culture," © 1980 The University of Michigan; several others were quoted in the introductory essay by Laurence Goldstein. The editors thank Mr. Goldstein for his cooperation and encouragement.

We are grateful to Reed Whittemore for contributing his valuable introduction to this volume and to Sally Troyer for her photographs.

We thank also those who brought to our attention poems that found their way into this collection: Upton Brady, Mary Ryan, Gladys Ely, and H.L. Van Brunt. To O.B. Hardison and Carol Burnes we owe gratitude for their helpful comments on earlier versions of this manuscript. And for her patience and perseverance, we thank Stacy Tuthill, publisher of the SCOP series, who first conceived the idea of an anthology of car poems. Special thanks to Jayne Silva, Katharine Zadravec and Stephanie Demma of the Editorial Board for their invaluable assistance in preparing this manuscript.

The Library of Congress has cataloged the first printing of this title as follows:

American classic : car poems for collectors / edited by Mary Swope & Walter H. Kerr ; introduction Reed Whittemore. — College Park, Md. : SCOP Publications, c1985.

　　　130 p. : ill. ; 23 cm.
　　　"SCOP eight."
　　　ISBN 0-930526-07-4 (pbk.) : $8.95

　　　1. American poetry—20th century.　2. Automobiles—Poetry.　I. Swope, Mary.　II. Kerr, Walter H., 1914-　　　III. Title: Car poems.

PS595.A87A48　　1985　　　　　　　　　　　　　　　　84-14061
　　　　　　　　　　811'.5'080356—dc19
　　　　　　　　　　　　　　　AACR 2　　MARC
Library of Congress

SCOP EIGHT in a series
Printed in the United States of America
SCOP Publications, Inc.
Box 376, College Park, Maryland 20740
Second Printing, February, 1987

Introduction

In the 19th century writers adjusted to the age of machines by practising on trains. Then Fords and Chevvies came in, and proved to be a great improvement over the monsters on tracks. The monsters could be listened to, watched, ridden on, but they couldn't be driven, or possessed—not at least by ordinary private persons like poets.

Fords and Chevvies also had the advantage of fitting the peculiar *virtu* of modern poets, their participatory itch; 19th century writers had begun to feel the itch, but it hadn't bothered them much. From a safe distance Emily Dickinson, for instance, could compare the power and precision of a train with those qualities in a good horse, and Thoreau could look across his pond at one and wonder why everybody was in a rush to get to Fitchburg. But the poets of this collection are characteristically like Denise Levertov and James Dickey (pp. 23, 55), whizzing along *with* their machines, and having, for better or worse, their destinies in hand as they do so.

Of course they may not have them well in hand. They may be satisfying a death wish, or driving blind into a traffic marker (see what is, perversely, my favorite poem in the book, Michael Casey's, on page 65); but they are usually somehow at home with their machines, feeling that the machines help them to take charge of their own affairs. The result for them as poets is that they don't have to sit on the sidelines being, merely, pundits, but can get up and go! A majority of the poems here are participatory in this sense.

There are fine exceptions, such as Howard Nemerov's "Fugue" and May Swenson's "Southbound on the Freeway". There are also hard-to-classify pieces that use a car as metaphor or analogue for something else (see Cummings and Bly, pp. 25, 14); but the main drift here is quite directly to describe a human soul and a machine soul achieving, oh lord, togetherness.

Small boats have sometimes played a similar role in literature, and there is of course Charles Lindbergh's book, *We*, about his romance with The Spirit of Saint Louis; but cars have had it all over boats and planes, as well as trains, as soul mates. *American Classic* is witness to the fact.

Some of the poets here are unhappy with their machines' souls, having a 19th century view of machines as evil forces in nature's garden; but the poets who are happy about them seem to feel that the machines are part of themselves. I'd say that the likers outnumber the haters, a good sign (though it is hard to take accurate count), and I'd say also the likers like their machines for their vices as well as their virtues, another good sign. David Barker's Packard (p. 19) is an extreme case, but a pleasant one. Who would substitute an anonymous shiny import for that fine old wreck? (I can see a few hands going up.)

I have a sad feeling that my own next car will be soulless and perfect, and will have a meaningless computer name like Izpay or Dabo. The cars of *American Classic* are not like that, and the machine age it represents may well soon seem, in comparison, idyllic.

Reed Whittemore

Contents

III

IV

V

Photographs
by
Sally Troyer

I

FUGUE

You see them vanish in their speeding cars,
The many people hastening through the world,
And wonder what they would have done before
This time of time speed distance, random streams
Of molecules hastened by what rising heat?
Was there never a world where people just sat still?

Yet they might be all of them contemplatives
Of a timeless now, drivers and passengers
In the moving cars all facing to the front
Which is the future, which is destiny,
Which is desire and desire's end—
What are they doing but just sitting still?

And still at speed they fly away, as still
As the road paid out beneath them as it flows
Moment by moment into the mirrored past;
They spread in their wake the parading fields of food,
The windowless works where who is making what,
The grey towns where the wishes and the fears are done.

COME WITH ME

Come with me into those things that have felt this despair for so
   long—
Those removed Chevrolet wheels that howl with a terrible loneliness,
Lying on their backs in the cindery dirt, like men drunk, and naked,
Staggering off down a hill at night to drown at last in the pond.
Those shredded inner tubes abandoned on the shoulders of thruways,
Black and collapsed bodies, that tried and burst,
And were left behind;
And the curly steel shavings, scattered about on garage benches,
Sometimes still warm, gritty when we hold them,
Who have given up, and blame everything on the government,
And those roads in South Dakota that feel around in the darkness . . .

PORTRAIT OF A MOTORCAR

It's a lean car . . . a long-legged dog of a car . . . a gray-ghost eagle
    car.
The feet of it eat the dirt of a road . . . the wings of it eat the hills.
Danny the driver dreams of it when he sees women in red skirts and
    red sox in his sleep.
It is in Danny's life and runs in the blood of him . . . a lean gray-ghost
    car.

THIS DIM AND PTOLEMAIC MAN

For forty years, for forty-one,
Sparing the profits of the sun,
This farmer piled his meagre hoard
To buy at last a rattly Ford.

Now crouched on a scared smile he feels
Motion spurt beneath his heels,
Rheumatically intent shifts gears,
Unloosens joints of rustic years.

Morning light obscures the stars,
He swerves avoiding other cars,
Wheels with the road, does not discern
He eastward goes at every turn,

Nor how his aged limbs are hurled
Through all the motions of the world,
How wild past farms, past ricks, past trees,
He perishes toward Hercules.

ASSEMBLY LINE

Henry had something on his mind
beyond the folderol of birds,
or horses waltzing in a field,
or loafing trees. Henry inclined
toward something practical and square,
and built it black and built it cheap
with wheels to last an average trip
(and, for emergencies, a spare).
Henry had hit on something new
to fill up dinner pails and time
and occupy men's noisy hands
and start a factory or two.

History was bunk, Henry averred
and turned a crank and set a spark,
honked at the corn and shimmied out
headlong across a neighing world;
plowed frogs and leaves and eagles under,
corrected mountains, fixed the dark,
followed a rainbow, found instead
the freeway's hot and surly thunder—
and at the end a twitching flare
like a red bush. History is junk.
Beneath, the earth is six feet deep;
the grass is optional and spare.

Karl Shapiro

BUICK

As a sloop with a sweep of immaculate wings on her delicate spine
And a keel as steel as a root that holds in the sea as she leans,
Leaning and laughing, my warm hearted beauty, you ride, you ride,
You tack on the curves with parabola speed and a kiss of goodbye,
Like a thoroughbred sloop, my new high-spirited spirit, my kiss.

As my foot suggests that you leap in the air with your hips of a girl,
My finger that praises your wheel and announces your voices of song,
Flouncing your skirts, you blueness of joy, you flirt of politeness,
You leap, you intelligence, essence of wheelness with silvery nose,
And your platinum blocks of excitement stir like the hairs of a fern.

But how alien you are from the booming belts of your birth and the
    smoke
Where you turned on the stinging lathes of Detroit and Lansing at
    night
And shrieked at the torch in your secret parts and the amorous tests,
But now with your eyes that enter the future of roads you forget;
You are all instinct with your phosphorous glow and your streaking
        hair.

And now when we stop it is not as the bird from the shell that I leave
Or the leathery pilot who steps from his bird with a sneer of delight,
And not as the ignorant beast do you squat and watch me depart,
But with exquisite breathing you smile, with satisfaction of love,
And I touch you again as you tick in the silence and settle in sleep.

David Barker

PACKARD

Once, new, you rolled easy and maroon
down a dry Arizona highway.

Somehow, like me, you came to Oregon. Picking up
a couple of coats of cream enamel along the way. I
too have turned a lighter shade.

That was when someone still cared enough
to fix a bashed fender and lead in a dented trunk.
But you moved to the deep woods and
fell on hard times.

I shall not rub salt in fresh wounds
telling sad stories of the sea air. Unwanted, you were
hauled by trailor from the coast to Salem
to turn over a quick buck.

But I, like some silly old lover, have
plucked the rotted cotton from your springs. I
bear you tender gifts of fiberglass, Rustoleum,
WD-40. I shall patch you up and make you anew,
my darling.

Together we shall travel very far indeed.

Albert Drake

1939 MERCURY

The first Merc built, and a convert—
all French curves, begging for lead.
I got the chrome off and saw
on winter nights, rain beating
like time on the top, huddled
over the radio, dash lights
warming our desires—
I saw it ground-hugging, smoothed
fenders, white leather inside,
Carson chopped top, and all below
painted purple, purple, a 1952 color.

I got the chrome off,
put the top down once—
otherwise we limped through the year
in primer-gray, rattles, a screaming
high gear, dead battery, water leaks.
See us:
boys with tight hard levis, loud shirts,
thin girls with sad wet hair;
on the corner we stand,
puffing damp cigarettes, smoke drifting
past neon like dreams
into the night.

IN A DREAM, THE AUTOMOBILE

                        Still accelerating,
my right foot useless, the needle passes
forty, forty-five, wavers at seventy, jumps,
is freed of numbers.
                        The beast flattens
to the road, belly filled with fire, feeds
on fire.   We roar into America,
tin mufflers belching on the western streets.
People stop, mouths suspended, stare,
are hurtled backwards.
                        They will remember
this myth of steel splitting the air on
either side making a passage of sound the
shriek of tires leaning at corners the mad
roaring of aluminum.
                        Our chrome dazzles
as we pass.

Into the mountains, the fantastic leaves glowing
in deadly colors. Past autumn. The thin air
sings above timberline.
                        At the top of America
we fly down. Valleys rush to meet us, turn
to night forests that gleam under the headlights.
As I fall asleep, distance and night close
and divide.

When I waken it has been morning for hours.
We have left the barrier mountains and
are rolling east into wheatfields.
The air swings at our side, the sun looms
in the large continent of yellow.
The tank, still full; a useless gauge.
Even the wheel does not respond but moves

according to the road. A farm breaks
the land, small settlements swell
in the distance and are gone. We sail
across the flat belly of America
towards the green edge of the Appalachians.
Between night and rain the deep forests
burn in lightning. A black rain
buries the road in thunder. There is
nothing beyond myself and this car
                    an engine meshing in secret
wheels turning to an invisible road
                    black waters.
                        Forward, faster,
the rain moving with us into morning,
into a sea of red clay, coastal sand,
until the breakers of the Atlantic
                    rise in one water
and we plunge, prison and passenger,
into the thunder!
                    America!

THE WAY THROUGH

Let the rain plunge radiant
through sulky thunder
rage on rooftops

let it scissor and bounce its denials
on concrete slabs and black
roadways. Flood the streets. It's much

but not enough, not yet: persist,
rain, real rain, sensuous,
swift, released from

       vague skies, the tedium
up there.

       Under scared bucking trees
the beach road washed out—

       trying to get by on the verge
       is no good, earth crumbles into the
       brown waterfall, but he backs up
the old car again and CHARGES.

The water flies in the halfwit's eyes
       who didn't move fast enough
"Who do you think I am, a horse?"
       but we made it—

       Drown us, lose us,
rain, let us loose, so,
to lose ourselves, to career
up the plunge of the hill

MOVING BETWEEN BELOIT AND MONROE

The car conveys us where we've been
because the scene discovers
over and over one simple green
to keep spring's mud and tubules covered.

Because the scene discovers
how grain bean grass and clover stir
to keep spring's mud and tubules covered,
the fields pass for one another.

How grain bean grass and clover stir!
Since newness grows everywhere the same,
the fields pass for one another
this month, murmuring its lovely name.

Since newness grows everywhere the same,
the car seems to stand still over
this month murmuring its lovely name
in permutations like a lover.

The car seems to stand still over—
over and over—one simple green
in permutations. Like a lover
the car conveys us where we've been.

she being Brand

-new;and you
know consequently a
little stiff i was
careful of her and(having

thoroughly oiled the universal
joint tested my gas felt of
her radiator made sure her springs were O.

K.)i went right to it flooded-the-carburetor cranked her

up,slipped the
clutch(and then somehow got into reverse she
kicked what
the hell)next
minute i was back in neutral tried and

again slo-wly;bare,ly nudg.   ing(my

lev-er Right-
oh and her gears being in
A 1 shape passed
from low through
second-in-to-high like
greasedlightning)just as we turned the corner of Divinity

avenue i touched the accelerator and give

her the juice,good

                              (it
was the first ride and believe i we was
happy to see how nice she acted right up to
the last minute coming back down by the Public
Gardens i slammed on
the

internalexpanding
&
externalcontracting
brakes Bothatonce and

brought allofher tremB
-ling
to a:dead.

stand-
;Still)

BIG CARS

Ten years later
they arrive on the thruway,
pulling winged fenders and smiling
a lane wide—big cars,
old floats that took a wrong
corner somewhere and lost
the American dream parade. Around them

the strange, grilleless
cars of the future
hum at their tires—tiny aliens
of a planet out of gas.

To think of their long trip
just beginning—the irrepressible fuel
rising everywhere into their tanks!
For the first time, armrests
unfolded out of seats;
out of the armrests, ashtrays!
Maps fell open to the new roads

which led them, finally, here
to the right lanes of America—
the antiques of optimism
nobody understands or wants
except the poor. Or dictators

driving down boulevards in some country
where the poor do not have cars
and run alongside until it seems
that they themselves are riding
on soft shocks, under a sun roof,
toward the great plenty of the New World.

THE AUTOMOBILE

It is the dark horse
and the easy rider
elemental choice and persuasion
drug-boot and foot-stone
and love affair
because it moves and roars
and leaves no room for rest.
The chase and hot pursuit,
tested skills of courage and evasion
and sexual thrust of " 'Drive, drive,'
he said" . . . and all, all of it
at the expense of love.
This is the only gift
the rich bequeath the poor . . .
the poor and unself-blessed
the brave ones here, masters of torque
and incendiary grief.
Their children hurtle onward and outward
through the Universe, braking only
on the curves.
They are riding the rain down on radials
and forging license plates
for the holy horse
they ride against the mothering earth.

I KNOW A MAN

And I sd to my
friend, because I am
always talking,—John, I

sd, which was not his
name, the darkness sur-
rounds us, what

can we do against
it, or else, shall we &
why not, buy goddamn big car,

drive, he sd, for
christ's sake, look
out where yr going.

RANDOM WHEELS

in l.a.
nobody
thinks about
driving
30 miles
for a good
party
or to see a
movie

the freeways
take you where
you want to go
you just play
the radio &
wait for your
car to find
the turnoff

nothing
could be easier

POETS HITCHHIKING ON THE HIGHWAY

Of course I tried to tell him
but he cranked his head
    without an excuse.
I told him the sky chases
    the sun
And he smiled and said:
    'What's the use.'
I was feeling like a demon
    again
So I said: 'But the ocean chases
    the fish.'
This time he laughed
    and said: 'Suppose the
        strawberry were
            pushed into a mountain.'
After that I knew the
    war was on—
So we fought:
He said: 'The apple-cart like a
            broomstick-angel
        snaps & splinters
                old dutch shoes.'
I said: 'Lightning will strike the old oak
        and free the fumes!'
He said: Mad street with no name.'

I said: 'Bald killer! Bald killer! Bald killer!'
He said, getting real mad,
        'Firestoves! Gas! Couch!'
I said, only smiling,
        'I know God would turn back his head
        if I sat quietly and thought.'
We ended by melting away,
    hating the air!

TÊTE-À-TÊTE

Lifting his slowly trickling jaws
from whip-laced roadside grass,
the horse creased back a thighlong neck
in time to see me driven past,
an amputated head
framed by auto glass.

But was he really seeing me,
before he sank his eggplant head
to graze again, or the steel green car
that made his stare look drunk,
as though a bolting tree trunk
had kicked some memory ajar?

WINDSHIELD

A wet day on the road: the slim blades cutting
Fans of transparency among water jewels;
Distension and rip of high-speed passers-by,
Deaf to the lowly gatherings of the field;
Corn tassels tossed and oak leaves flowing in
    darkening
Grey rain and western wind.
                      Unplug the lighter
And frown cross-eyed upon that fiery circlet;
There is always something wanting about our hands,
On just-soft cushions lolling or lightly at work
With the slender wheel; and there is something
Perpetually unsaid in what we say—
Our silken exhalations of being friends.
A failure of no consequence?
                    I've dreamed
Of armless men in carnivals, legless men
Knuckling like apes on smoky avenues,
A world's whole host of savage crippled men
Silent but for the single cry: "Somewhere!"

On each long curve the highway balances
Against our speed with tight terrestrial power,
Conducting to no other place but here;
Here always, the wide alien light of home,
The ever-present wildness of the air—
The nightly dread, say, in cold parishes
Of some tall silvery and unsmiling Father—
A child's wish to do something simply superb.

Paul Zimmer

DRIVING NORTH FROM SAVANNAH
ON MY BIRTHDAY

Surely most signs pass me by unnoticed;
Not the squares and octagons of the road,
But twirls of scud, magic rings of fungi,
Marks that tree limbs scribble
On the sky, subtle dances of insects,
Veerings of flocks of birds,
Things that form and point to me—
Signs that might have shown me
How to live the rest of my life.

Forty-four years old today.
I think, too, of the minutes I have lived.
Twenty-two million yellow butterflies
Migrating south, sailing and turning,
Tying intricate knots over the road.
I wipe them out by the thousands,
Driving my car hard north
Against their fragile yearnings.

THIS DARKNIGHT SPEED

Sometimes I feel about love
like driving places at darknight speed
with the radio on,
doing what the saxophone
was barking in the bar:
"better yet, better yet, better get in a car!"

Sometimes I forget
simple words like rapture
for this animal joy,
this sense of being up to speed
and merging from a ramp,
knowing the driver in the mirror
is already adjusting to meet me
and wants it to go smooth,
wants me to have my turn,
not break acceleration
or miss a beat,

wants to meet and make a dance of it
at such a speed,
if you can imagine,
at such a speed that eyes tear from wind
blowing music out the windows.

I always believe
I could start pacing with somebody
on a long highway,
playing all the fast songs
and looking at the truck stops
for that one car

because sometimes I'm lonely
or I need to feel alive
or I just like being on the road in a car,
in a marvelous, monstrous killer-machine
that fills a human body crazy high
on landscape flying by the windows—
just a blur, just a shot of speed.

I always believe
I could get myself in somebody's eyes
wide and interstate-steady,
just flat out speeding along
and scanning the road ahead,
wanting to drive
like that
forever

and if I could keep it up,
god, if I could keep that up

I'd go absolutely right straight crazy to heaven

NOSTALGIA FOR 70

I think I could live at seventy miles an hour
traveling south like this forever, trees slipping
past on either side of the car while the farthest
green fields, keeping pace a little longer, fall
slowly behind as the grille eats miles of gray concrete
or forages for gnats like a whale in a shrimpbed.

It's easy calling a different room each evening home.
For when we are home, behind those mountains at our back,
trees and fields are always falling past our windows,
the house whines like an engine held at seventy, and evenings
we come to the same room a little further south.

And if, there at home, each morning before we pull
away, fields and fencerows back of the house
stand motionless, it's only because they are keeping pace:
house and field are holding steady like two cars
side by side at seventy on an endless interstate.

And though we seem to stand, we know we are traveling
steadily south, the weather is growing pleasanter,
and we are entering a season of orange groves.
Every day now for many days, perhaps for years,
ocean will lie on the horizon, a destination.

Coco Gordon

SECTION 14 FROM SUITE FOR JOHN CAGE
FOR THE PIANO-TRAP

It is on film.
In the dream when a mirage
intends to trap
you turn yourself
into a buoy—
you have just driven 400 miles a day
two days.
The road moves at 55 miles per hour
a pleat in the road
if you reach it your car will be swallowed.
You cannot stop
but the film slips.
There you are
on it with your yellow Fiesta
anchored to it.
This is the room, hands oarlocked,
in which you will work.

SLOW DRIVERS

Smug
or timid
not always the old
behind the wheel
they sit right
in the middle of the Law
as if it belongs to them;
as if they will inherit
what's yours as well
with your life;
keep you behind them
on narrow roads
hours, days
it seems
all your life!
as if it belongs to them;
it's not that you're reckless
or foolish
or would have them
that way, equally dangerous;
but you must be getting on, getting on
not loitering behind them
where they bait
your fury
and impatience across double lines
into blind
curves
making you wait
wait
wait
wait
wait until you savor the heady salt
of risk on the palate
and pull out

seeing death
in their eyes
when they smirk
at you
as you
pass

REMEMBERING THE AUTOMOBILE

Every so often he climbs into his car. And settling down
to the wheel, jams the accelerator. He begins to find

the houses he dreamed an evening before—beside the bridge
he buckled beneath several years past. Now the hint

of his mortal immortality takes hold. The manifest rises
through the delicate hairs of the chimney smoke and speaks,

from out the mouths of puzzlers who slide to dark corners
where they await an unsuspecting lout from the next house.

Or hang from the cliffs of their car windows stopping time
with unconsidered vigor. As time rises and falls

like whitewater streams of Yellowstone that gurgle through
fossil remains to surface in a sudden swerve. O the stories

that pass through the mind on this occasion! The beauties
of ripeness that flutter and flap in quixotic arrangement!

You see, our friend knows that life was meant for him,
so that when he places the little revolver under his pillow,

he understands exactly why. And can scrape easily the face
from the rear view mirror, as he displaces the encumbering material,

a kind of *summa acrobatica* that collapses with her hard tongue.
That re-enters as the children spill from the open car doors.

AS ANIMALS

Green New Hampshire
on the road and the radio playing.
Behind each thicket
crickets like irritation

part the air.
This car divides the road.
I drive the uncombed side:
the grasses waver,

little splashes of gravel sprout.
Blue car in the blue air,
I am hurrying somewhere
fifty miles an hour while,

roadside, from each stalk of grass,
a microcosm watches, wondering.
Each froth of spittle
on the vetch hides complex

compound eyes.
Each gall, inside, is star-
shaped, cancer-weird:
a smug worm, cradled, watches.

Trees along the shoulder
stand up beside the road,
slim organ pipes,
their water driven upward.

It is soundless for them, fingering
the wind, like practicing.
And I am practicing
being independent, greedy

through the country,
swallowing the green of it
and speeding—
Where's the stop?—

to some unproven mountain top
as if to choose one view
while the ground breathes,
heaving upward,

and a sweet sunlit smell
rushes in the car windows
like small strawberries, wild,
like lying in a meadow,

parting the leaves, and finding
them. Now the mountains
bump against me,
the hills tumble together;

the trees are racing me
to the waterfalls
and the road cuts the edges
of gulleys

and the radio is twanging:
be American.
Drive forever!—
I downshift at the curves.

Live forever.
The mind is suspended.
Driving is a sensation
unending, cool as sunset,

slowing finally by some
unnamed meadow, the clover darkening,
the sun finishing, the car huddled,
watching, inert: silent as animals.

ROCK AND ROLL

Rock and Roll split the head of Gospel, burst out
mean as Athena from the brain of Zeus,
stuck his thumb in the eye of Rhythm and Blues,
and hitched a ride up the river in a Caddy that was
w   i   d   e
and wicked as the Mississippi,
tap dancin' ALL OVER the red velvet seats.
shakin' his tight lil' punk ass out the window,
curdlin' the Dairy Queens.
He was bendin' his G-string, keepin' his back-beat,
blowin' up the city on his big long gol-den horn.
Rock and Roll was comin' to GET YOU!

He was the boogie man in the closet, shakin' in there w/yr
mittens and yr girl scout badge and yr red rubber boots,
stitchin' up the hem on yr communion dress w/Chantilly lace.
Rock and Roll was
HAPPENIN'
like chords screechin' along yr chalkboard,
like yr pencil against yr inkwell.
Rock and Roll was walkin' the dog
across yr teacher's hair-sprayed head.
The Nina, the Pinta, and the Santa Maria were bouncin' BANG
into Plymouth Rock, the Pilgrims were reelin' and
everybody rolled the Injuns.
You knew it.
You knew it was true what Rock and Roll said.
You could hear him talkin' off the windows, all those
hot radios in the school parking lot, all those pistons
comin' in at the upbeat. Rock and Roll was

OUT THERE

HE WAS WAITIN' FOR YOU! Layin' right upside the school door,
scratchin' a thick old kitchen match on school brick,
tappin' a Marlboro out of his t-shirt.

ROCK AND ROLL

all zippers and grease and black black leather
flashin' out of yr closet and gobblin' up yr mother
like some bad baaaaaaaad wolf.

ROCK AND ROLL HAS BEEN COMIN' YR WAY—cruisin' Main
    Street,
makin' an il-legal left down New Jersey, sittin' on his horn
through every red/stop in the Bronx.
Rock and Roll is steamin' out the windows, lettin' in the breeze,
comin' to curl yr locks w/hot licks, baaa-bay.

Rock and Roll is out there loungin' in the spotlight of yr
corner streetlamp, jammin' w/yr good goodnight angels,
mentionin' a groove in yr sweet little dreams.

ROCK AND ROLL IS UNDER YR BED!

He is comin' to let you dance, little sister, comin' to
put the strut in yr stuff, the bend
in yr dimpled knee. He is slittin' his wrists
to bleed yr best dress red, he is SACRIFICIN'—cuttin' out his heart
just to give you a beat.

Rock and Roll is leanin' on yr school bell, one, two, three, FOR
    YOU,
w/his hot lips wrapped around a grin big as Montana,
w/his old Ford door WIDE OPEN on that
Promised Land.

Joan Retallack

SOUTHERN LIEBESLIEDER

Hoch, hoch sind die Berge, usw.   Schumann

1.

The sun stubs itself out in the hills.
What could be more "Southern" than that?
Won't you come back, Lily Dale? Cars move
their fins across its obese grave. And us
up to our knees, past nutrition
in these itchy grasses, never scratching.
Pass the pastels, s'il vous plait. *High,*
high are the mountains, etc.
How steep is the path, etc.

2.

Already the azaleas have begun to rust.
What could be more "Germanic" than that?
Am I a fooo-oo-oo-oo-oool for loving you?
The sun stubs itself out in the hills.
Pass the burnt ochre, s'il vous plait.
Why won't those damned petals fall?
Brazen exhibitionists! They blow
Death's wrinkled genitals candy kisses.
The sun stubs itself out in the hills
achieving high mathematical probability.
Between love and death lies high
mathematical probability. *High, high*
are the mountains, etc.

3.

The happiness is gone/ The heartaches linger on
achieving high mathematical probability. This
splendid Palladian window informs the view
as electric saws sing into the trees, rivaling
the Carbonated Warbler. Between love and death
lies the Palladian window it would seem
as the sun stubs itself out in one's face
and other embarrassments accrue despite
soft, wraith-like hints of Spring.
O steep is the path, etc.

4.
The sun garrotes itself in the wisteria.
I've got your picture/ She's got you.
There's more to the South than wisteria
she says with her Kentucky neon smile.
The sun's dorsal fin slinks into the sea. Fuck-
ing among the ruins gives us a sense— Already
the azaleas have begun to rust. Dusty sows
skirt the corn's stubble.
Indigo has dyed this island blue.
Far from the hills (*Low,*
low is the low-country, etc.)
the Apostolic Bus rides syncopated rhythms
designed to fracture melancholy. The sun
stalls in Caw Caw Swamp. The crow
haws in Caw Caw Swamp, etc.

5.
From a Georgian piazza in Charleston,
"the South's most deliberately civilized city,"
the sun drowns itself in the harbor.
Soft, wraith-like tints tint the slicks.
Not much is playing at the flicks—
King Kong, Swiss Family Robinson.
The Carbonated Warbler sings its fizzy song,
shits indigo on white balustrades.
Already the azaleas have begun to rust.
Cedar Waxwings bash the too-clean panes.
Deep within I bear my pain, etc.
Soft, wraith-like scents seep from the mills
riding a low-country breeze.
O steep is the path, etc.

6.
Already the sun has begun to rust.
What is figurative in the North is literal
in the South, no/yes? Deliberate
octogenarians scale fragile helices
to wind despotic clocks, rest in the nape
like snails. Steeping in Jasmine tea, soggy
petals unfurl wan smiles at afternoon tea
smiling through— Art/Life, Life/Death, Death/Love,   49

Hand/Glove, etc. "These unfashionable
dichotomies make me sneeze," *O
steep is the path*, "Bless you," etc.
And all around, PECANS, FIREWORKS & GAS,
FREE SHOES FOR LIFE, SOUTHERN MASSAGE.
*It's a long, long way from the tips of your fingers
to what I feel in my heart. High, high
are the mountains, etc.*

COUNTRY SINGER

She keeps her voice
in a tin cup
high in her mouth
and ladles it over the rim
letting it flow
like river music, easy water,
fingernail moon in the sky,
the trickling sound
trees would make

if they had voices,
telephone poles
like pitchforks
tuned at a sky
where wires rise
and fall in scallops,
skirthems swooning
lifting for the only man
she ever loved.

A capella now, they travel
octaves apart, flute water,
fiddle water, manwater,
womanstain, the woman
in one house, the man
in another, bad booze
or a lover between for the love
of incredible longing.

But we are riding
down this road together
to the throb
of turning wheels, moving
in steel through darkness
carrying ahead of us
our twin bouquets of light.

Wallace Stevens

REALITY IS AN ACTIVITY
OF THE MOST AUGUST IMAGINATION

Last Friday, in the big light of last Friday night,
We drove home from Cornwall to Hartford, late.

It was not a night blown at a glassworks in Vienna
Or Venice, motionless, gathering time and dust.

There was a crush of strength in a grinding going round,
Under the front of the westward evening star,

The vigor of glory, a glittering in the veins,
As things emerged and moved and were dissolved,

Either in distance, change or nothingness,
The visible transformations of summer night,

An argentine abstraction approaching form
And suddenly denying itself away.

There was an insolid billowing of the solid.
Night's moonlight lake was neither water nor air.

III

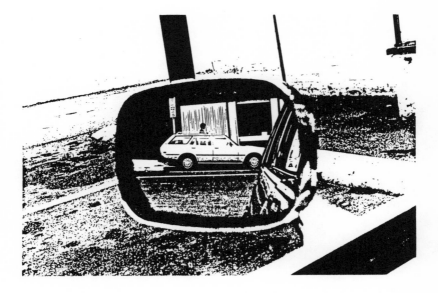

CHERRYLOG ROAD

Off Highway 106
At Cherrylog Road I entered
The '34 Ford without wheels,
Smothered in kudzu,
With a seat pulled out to run
Corn whiskey down from the hills,

And then from the other side
Crept into an Essex
With a rumble seat of red leather
And then out again, aboard
A blue Chevrolet, releasing
The rust from its other color,

Reared up on three building blocks.
None had the same body heat;
I changed with them inward, toward
The weedy heart of the junkyard,
For I knew that Doris Holbrook
Would escape from her father at noon

And would come from the farm
To seek parts owned by the sun
Among the abandoned chassis,
Sitting in each in turn
As I did, leaning forward
As in a wild stock-car race

In the parking lot of the dead.
Time after time, I climbed in
And out the other side, like
An envoy or movie star
Met at the station by crickets.
A radiator cap raised its head,

Become a real toad or a kingsnake
As I neared the hub of the yard,
Passing through many states,
Many lives, to reach
Some grandmother's long Pierce-Arrow
Sending platters of blindness forth

From its nickel hubcaps
And spilling its tender upholstery
On sleepy roaches,
The glass panel in between
Lady and colored driver
Not all the way broken out,

The back-seat phone
Still on its hook.
I got in as though to exclaim,
"Let us go to the orphan asylum,
John; I have some old toys
For children who say their prayers."

I popped with sweat as I thought
I heard Doris Holbrook scrape
Like a mouse in the southern-state sun
That was eating the paint in blisters
From a hundred car tops and hoods.
She was tapping like code,

Loosening the screws,
Carrying off headlights,
Sparkplugs, bumpers,
Cracked mirrors and gear-knobs,
Getting ready, already,
To go back with something to show

Other than her lips' new trembling
I would hold to me soon, soon,
Where I sat in the ripped back seat
Talking over the interphone,
Praying for Doris Holbrook
To come from her father's farm

And to get back there
With no trace of me on her face
To be seen by her red-haired father
Who would change, in the squalling barn,
Her back's pale skin with a strop,
Then lay for me

In a bootlegger's roasting car
With a string-triggered 12-gauge shotgun
To blast the breath from the air.
Not cut by the jagged windshields,
Through the acres of wrecks she came
With a wrench in her hand,

Through dust where the blacksnake dies
Of boredom, and the beetle knows
The compost has no more life.
Someone outside would have seen
The oldest car's door inexplicably
Close from within:

I held her and held her and held her,
Convoyed at terrific speed
By the stalled, dreaming traffic around us,
So the blacksnake, stiff
With inaction, curved back
Into life, and hunted the mouse

With deadly overexcitement,
The beetles reclaimed their field
As we clung, glued together,
With the hooks of the seat springs
Working through to catch us red-handed
Amidst the gray breathless batting

That burst from the seat at our backs.
We left by separate doors
Into the changed, other bodies
Of cars, she down Cherrylog Road
And I to my motorcycle
Parked like the soul of the junkyard

Restored, a bicycle fleshed
With power, and tore off
Up Highway 106, continually
Drunk on the wind in my mouth,
Wringing the handlebar for speed,
Wild to be wreckage forever.

DRIVING CARL'S '56 CHEVY

It really isn't much of a car.
You sit high up like in a truck
and the clutch comes up forever before it grabs.
But driving down Harding Highway alone,
suddenly I am Duke Proud,
racing the cops, betting the guys
they can't grab a buck off the dashboard
when I hit second.
Then Jo Ann Richmond is close
beside me on the seat, saying,
"I told my parents we were going to the dance,
but I bet I can guess where you want to go."
She has big tits for fifteen
and that's my ring around her neck
on the strongest chain in the world.

THE JESUS INFECTION

Jesus is with me
on the Blue Grass Parkway going eastbound.
He is with me
on the old Harrodsburg Road coming home.
I am listening
to country gospel music
in the borrowed Subaru.
The gas pedal
and the words
leap to the music.
O throw out the lifeline!
Someone is drifting away.

Flags fly up in my mind
without my knowing
where they've been lying furled
and I am happy
living in the sunlight
where Jesus is near.
A man is driving his polled Herefords
across the gleanings of a cornfield
while I am bound for the kingdom of the free.
At the little trestle bridge that has no railing
I see that I won't have to cross Jordan alone.

Signposts every mile exhort me
to Get Right With God
and I move over.
There's a neon message blazing
at the crossroad
catty-corner to the Burger Queen:
Ye Come With Me.
It is well with my soul, Jesus?
It sounds so easy
to be happy after the sunrise,
to be washed in the crimson flood.

Now I am tailgating
and I read a bumper sticker
on a Ford truck full of Poland Chinas.
It says: Honk If You Know Jesus
and I do it.
My sound blats out for miles
behind the pigsqueal
and it's catching in the front end,
in the axle,
in the universal joint,
this rich contagion.

We are going down the valley on a hairpin turn,
the swine and me, we're breakneck in
we're leaning on
the everlasting arms.

RIDING WITH THE FIREWORKS

down Mississippi Route 61 to catch up
with the American Wind Symphony Barge

We are bouncing along in the blue
van trying to catch the barge
that ran by Greenville at 10 AM
and kept on traveling down
that center channel going like a bat
out of Helena Arkansas. The lower
the river, the faster the channel
                    flows.

We have just passed
the road to Hushkapena
and I know for a fact
I will never go there.

Lou takes out his
bass trombone
to show me how
a circular valve
differs from a piston,
and tells me how
his steel co-workers
differ from
musicians
who never would have called him
Trombone Lou.

Here at the Yazoo River, at
Vicksburg where the wrecked train cars
are still crumpled on one track,
where the Atlas Tank Co.'s sign says
"EVERYTHING" on its storage shed,
we are stopped by the Illinois Central Gulf
switching its piggy-back cars. At the River Store
the sign says "POSITIVELY NO CHILDREN OR VISITORS

OR ███████ BEYOND THIS POINT." Could the
blackened blank read FIREWORKS underneath?

Under the front seat of the van,
under a Gideon Bible
are the signs: red letters
exploding on white:
    EXPLOSIVES
In my pocket are
my cigarettes. I clutch
the matches tight.
Hushkapena has become
(for me) (unknown to it)
the place I'll go
if we roll this van
into those final fireworks.

Down the river, around
the bend, riding low
water on its high pitch
comes the silver barge,
an enormous flute
for a latter day Paul Bunyan.
Grabbing our suitcases
and the groceries,
we lurch down the river bank
where the earth is separating
in jagged angles.
We board the board across
flowing water to the first moving barge
crawl around the outer narrow ledge
laced with chicken feed
and make the final leap
onto the silver lady,
Point Counterpoint
the Second, just as
the C# moon strikes
a chord across
the sunset clef, and all
    is music, music.

WHO'S IN CHARGE HERE?

I saw him hanging from the cab window,
bent at the waist, and I braked alongside.
He had just jackknifed onto the shoulder
and he was drunk and he was tired and he

was late to Chicago with perishables.
Someone stopped and brought out a thermos
of coffee. He didn't mind. It didn't
change a thing. He took in his awkward arms

the whole grill of that worthy mammoth
and kissed it and said, "I take good care
of her and she takes care of me,"
and put his mouth to it and pushed his chest to it

like a prisoner against his bars
but mostly like a trucker on a timetable
in a rig that could mostly have its way
with any thinking man with a tuft of good sense.

I didn't say, "Look out where you're going."
He would. He shook my hand hard, showing me.
Then he became his truck again, and I my car
to cross a river—that's where the highway was going.

DRIVING WHILE UNDER THE INFLUENCE

it was three A.M. and I hit
the blinking yellow light
on the route three rotary at Drum Hill
we got out quick to throw away beer cans
and then I tried to drive forward
but the car wouldn't go forward
so I backed up around the rotary
off of it and into a gas station
I figured I could put my car
in the row of cars already parked there
and nobody would notice   right?
I gets out and hides behind
by this time I can see the flashing lights
and it was something to watch
the cruiser goes around the rotary slow
takes the exit I took
and comes straight to me
I was alone all my friends split
and they got me for leaving the scene
driving while under the influence
and being a minor in possession
all kinds of stuff right?
I asked the guy caught me
how'd you find me
how'd you find me
he said he followed the leaking radiator
it leaked after the crash right?
fifty million dumb cops in the world
and this one has to be a genius

IN THE BLACK CAMARO

Through the orange glow of taillights, I crossed
the dirt road, entered the half-mile
of darkness and owl screech, tangled briar
and fallen trunk,
followed the yellow beam of Billy Parker's flashlight
down the slick needle-hill,
half crawling, half sliding and kicking
for footholds, tearing up
whole handfuls of scrub brush and leaf-mulch
until I jumped the mud bank, walked the ankle-deep creek,
the last patch of pine, the gully,
and knelt at the highway
stretching in front of Billy Parker's house,
spotted the black Chevy Camaro parked under a maple
not fifty feet from the window
where Billy Parker rocked in and out of view,
studied in the bad light of a table lamp
the fine print of his Allstate policy.

I cut the flashlight, checked up and down the highway.
Behind me the screech growing distant, fading
into woods, but coming on
a network of tree frogs signaling along the creek.
Only that, and the quiet of my heels
coming down on asphalt
as I crossed the two-lane and stood at the weedy edge
of Billy Parker's yard, stood
in the lamp glare of the living room
where plans were being made to make me rich
and thought of a boat and Johnson outboard,
of all the lures on a K-Mart wall, of reels
and graphite rods, coolers of beer, weedy banks
of dark fishy rivers,
and of Billy Parker rocking in his chair,
studying his coverage, his bank account,
his layoff at Lockheed, his wife laboring
in the maternity ward of the Cobb General Hospital.

For all of this, I crouched in the shadow of fender
and maple, popped the door on the Camaro,
and found in the faint house-light drifting
through the passenger's window
the two stripped wires hanging below the dash.
I took the driver's seat, kicked the clutch,
then eased again as I remembered
the glove box and the pint of Seagram's Billy Parker
had not broken the seal on. Like an alarm
the tree frogs went off in the woods. I drank
until they hushed
and I could hear through stray cricket chatter
the rockers on Billy Parker's chair
grinding ridges into his living room floor, worry
working on him like hard time. Then a wind
working in river grass, a red current
slicing around stumps and river snags, a boat-drift
pulling against an anchor
as I swayed in the seat of the black Camaro, grappled
for the two wires hanging in the darkness
between my knees, saw through the tinted windshield
by a sudden white moon rolling out of the clouds
a riverbank two counties away,
a wooden bridge, a place to jump
and roll on the soft shoulder of the gravel road,
a truck backed into a thicket a half-mile downstream.

WHIPLASH

That month he was broke,
so when the brakes to his car
went sloshy, he let them go.
Next month his mother came
to visit, and out they went
to gawk, to shop, to have something
to do while they talked besides
sitting down like a seminar
to talk. One day soon he'd fix
the brakes, or—as he joked
after nearly bashing a cab
and skidding widdershins
through the intersection
of Viewcrest and Edgecliff—
they'd fix him, one of these
oncoming days. We like
to explain our lives to ourselves,
so many of our fictions
are about causality—chess
problems (where the *?!* after
White's 16th move marks
the beginning of disaster),
insurance policies, box scores,
psychotherapy ("Were your
needs being met in this
relationship?"), readers' guides
to pity and terror—, and about
the possibility that because
aging is relentless, logic too
runs straight and one way only.

By this hope to know how
our disasters almost shatter us,
it would make sense to say
the accident he drove into
the day after his mother left

began the month he was broke.
Though why was he broke?
Because of decisions he'd made
the month before to balance
decisions the month before that,
and so on all the way back
to birth and beyond, for his
mother and father brought
to his life the luck of theirs.

And so when his car one slick day
oversped its dwindling ability
to stop itself and smacked two
parked cars and lightly kissed
another, like a satisfying
billiards shot, and all this action
(so slow in compression and
preparation) exploded so quickly,
it seemed not that his whole life
swam or skidded before him,
but that his whole life was behind
him, like a physical force,
the way a dinosaur's body
was behind its brain and the news
surged up and down its vast
and clumsy spine like an early
version of the blues; indeed,
indeed, what might he do
but sing, as if to remind himself
by the power of anthem that the body's
disparate and selfish provinces
are connected. And that's how
the police found him, full-throated,
dried blood on his white suit
as if he'd been caught in a rust-
storm, song running back and forth
along his hurt body like the action
of a wave, which is not water,
strictly speaking, but a force
that water welcomes and displays.   69

LOST PARENTS

It takes a fast car
                    to lead a double life
in these days of short-distance love affairs
    when he has far-out lovers in
                            three different locations
    and a date with each one
                    at least twice a week
a little simple arithmetic shows
        what a workout he's engaged in
crossing & recrossing the city
        from bedroom to patio to swimming pool
the ignition key hot
    and the backseat a jumble of clothes
                        for different life-styles
a surfboard on the roof
    and a copy of Kahlil Gibran or Rod McKuen
                    under the dashboard
        next to the Indian music cassettes
packs of Tarot and the I-Ching
                  crammed into the glove compartment
    along with old traffic tickets
                  and hardpacks of Kents
        dents attesting to the passion
                of his last lover
And his answering service
        catching him on the freeway
            between two calls or two encounter groups
    and the urgent message left

with an unlisted number to call Carol
    about the bottle of fine wine
        he forgot to pick up
            and deliver to the gallery
                for the reception at nine

While she shuttles to her gynecologist
            and will meet him later
                    between two other numbers
                                    male or female
        including his wife
                who also called twice
wanting to know where he's been
            and what he's done
                    with their throw-away children
        who
                left to their own devices
                            in a beach house at Malibu
        grew up and dropped out into Nothing
            in a Jungian search
                        for lost parents
                            their own age

Josephine Miles

REASON

Said, Pull her up a bit will you, Mac, I want to unload there
Said, Pull her up my rear end, first come first serve.
Said, Give her the gun, Bud, he needs a taste of his own bumps.
Then the usher came out and got into the act:

Said, Pull her up, pull her up a bit, we need this space, sir.
Said, For God's sake, is this still a free country or what?
You go back and take care of Gary Cooper's horse
And leave me handle my own car.

Saw them unloading the lame old lady,
Parked out under the wheel and gave her an elbow,
Said, All you needed to do was just explain;
Reason, Reason is my middle name.

IV

AGREEABLE MONSTERS

What calls itself Crane
but is quite clearly Giraffe
above the midriff, where a
breathing light twitches—
bolt-eyed, iron-eared,
neck an extensible
stalk, a feed-bag-sized
hook painted orange
hung under the chin
or dropped loadward
by cables unwound from
inside like a spider's:
                    a towtruck,
hind-quarter-lights pulsing
as dragonflies do, or fireflies,
occasionally seen towing
another towtruck:
                    a revolving
cement-mixer, one of a herd
from a barn up near Co-op City,
whose Tilt-a-Whirl paunch's
pink, blue and magenta
polka-dots may be
trying to tell us
something:
                the daily dog-walker's
straining bouquet-on-a-leash:
three poodles, two St.
Bernards, a Doberman,
a Schnauzer:
                such
agreeable monsters go
up and down Third Avenue.

May Swenson

SOUTHBOUND ON THE FREEWAY

A tourist came in from Orbitville,
parked in the air, and said:

The creatures of this star
are made of metal and glass.

Through the transparent parts
you can see their guts.

Their feet are round and roll
on diagrams or long

measuring tapes, dark
with white lines.

They have four eyes.
The two in back are red.

Sometimes you can see a five-eyed
one, with a red eye turning

on the top of his head.
He must be special—

the others respect him
and go slow

when he passes, winding
among them from behind.

They all hiss as they glide,
like inches, down the marked

tapes. Those soft shapes,
shadowy inside

the hard bodies—are they
their guts or their brains?

MERRITT PARKWAY

As if it were
forever that they move, that we
keep moving—

    Under a wan sky where
    as the lights went on a star
       pierced the haze and now
    follows steadily
              a constant
    above our six lanes
    the dreamlike continuum . . .

    And the people — ourselves!
      the humans from inside the
      cars, apparent
      only at gasoline stops
                  unsure,
         eyeing each other

            drink coffee hastily at the
            slot machines and hurry
        back to the cars
        vanish
        into them forever, to
        keep moving —

And the people — ourselves!

Houses now and then beyond the
sealed road, the trees / trees, bushes
passing by, passing
    the cars that
       keep moving ahead of

    us, past us, pressing behind us
                   and
           over left, those that come
         toward us shining too brightly
moving relentlessly

      in six lanes, gliding
      north and south, speeding with
      a slurred sound —

Laura McLaughlin

BELTWAY

Released from the stop
and go of the streets,
round our cities
jeweled belts
whirl at twilight
like necklaces twirled—
diamonds one way,
rubies the other.

for Robert Phillips

If you stare long enough perhaps it becomes beautiful.
If you translate its colors into comedy sounds—
ochre, russet, coppery-pink, nutmeg—
perhaps it becomes merely an anti-world,
another way of seeing.

An industrial slum gaily glaring
in a mid-summer squall:
porous smoke rising heavy and leaden-pale as a giant's limbs,
the sickly air heaving in gusts,
sulphurous blooms whipping in the wind.
Here, an ancient sea-bed
guarded by a twelve-foot chain link fence.
Clouds break companionably about the highest smokestacks.
Factory windows, opaque with grime, slant open
into the 100° shade.
You stare, you memorize, you do not wish to judge.
Your lungs shrink shy of the bold air.

Scars' stitchings in the earth,
high-tension wires whining thinly overhead.
What is there to say about what we see,
what is the compulsion to make judgments,
to invent visions?

This is the base of the pyramid, of course.
But it is not strewn with workers' bones:
it glowers and winks with their acres of parked cars.
If the air is noxious perhaps it is you who have weakened.

It is you who wonder what creatures graze in such pastures,
brood beside such rancid ponds—
giant crab-spiders of wire and rust,
toads with swollen white bellies,
armoured things with spiny tails and eyes
staring unperturbed at the ends of stalks.
It is you who observe most of *Ford* obscured by filth:
And you who see again at the top of the highest smokestack
the same plastic wreath you'd seen at Christmas,
wondering if it was a joke:
Joy to the World   Gilmore Chemicals.

What is there to say about what we see,
what we cannot not see?

FILLING STATION

Oh, but it is dirty!
—this little filling station,
oil-soaked, oil-permeated
to a disturbing, over-all
black translucency.
Be careful with that match!

Father wears a dirty,
oil-soaked monkey suit
that cuts him under the arms,
and several quick and saucy
and greasy sons assist him
(it's a family filling station),
all quite thoroughly dirty.

Do they live in the station?
It has a cement porch
behind the pumps, and on it
a set of crushed and grease-
impregnated wickerwork;
on the wicker sofa
a dirty dog, quite comfy.

Some comic books provide
the only note of color—
of certain color. They lie
upon a big dim doily
draping a taboret
(part of the set), beside
a big hirsute begonia.

Why the extraneous plant?
Why the taboret?
Why, oh why, the doily?
(Embroidered in daisy stitch
with marguerites, I think,
and heavy with gray crochet.)

81

Somebody embroidered the doily.
Somebody waters the plant,
or oils it, maybe. Somebody
arranges the rows of cans
so that they softly say:
ESSO — SO - SO - SO
to high-strung automobiles.
Somebody loves us all.

THIS YEAR

I've slept in five houses, but wakened
in one body over and over. My eyes
stung by headlights, sore-boned
at the struggling wheel, I've steered
our goods through each bad weather.
Now our blood's jazzed again
on thin air; the money's ample,
the Rockies huge. We feel
on our way somewhere.

And yet, I ache at how dreams
can swerve to a cliff-edge, wheels
holding barely . . . I think
how prodigal longings are (sparks
echoed in a house of mirrors), how far
from home our destinations: Han-shan
high on Cold Mountain; Lowell
struck down in his cab.

1977

COUNTRY DRIVE-IN

Sudden around the curve a high-up and huge
face luminous as a clock blocks out a quarter-sky.
Small I move small in my small car below
the head of a giantess, unbodied as John's
on the screen's charger.
Blue as seas, its eyes release bright pools,
kidney-shaped tears slide down the vasty cheeks.
The lips' cavern parts on teeth
whiter and bigger than any bedded wolf's.
How can I fit her mammoth grief
into the dark below my matchstick ribs?

WHEN WE DRIVE AT NIGHT

When we drive at night
the houses shy away from the roads
or else they huddle together
confused, in the empty spaces.
The rush of so much longing is what they fear.

We ache when we drive
like the smashed Mack truck, abandoned by the side of the road,
which flashes its one red blinker
and continues to shriek for help: I want! I want!
From the dumps the tires are calling
softly, like mouths, in the rain.

And there are lives like this.
In our cars late at night, we are bigamists, nervous and aging,
saddened by wives.
We become that bus driver
who started out after lunch and drove to Nicaragua.

Who knows what we wish?
Watching you drive beside me,
I think of all the dark windows of automobiles,
the children asleep in the back,
and I picture the mind, unknown,
as hidden in caverns of the body
as the ghosts in these machines.

All night our eyes are full
of small black shadows on roads
that trail off into the back country and are lost.

SKELETON KEY

Opening and starting key for a
1954 Dodge junked last year

```
          O with what key
         shall I unlock this
        heart Tight in a coffer
       of chest something awaits a
      jab a click a sharp turn yes an
     opening Out with it then Let it
    pour into forms it molds itself
   Much like an escape of dreaming
  prisoners taking shape out in a
 relenting air in bright volumes
unimaginable even amid anterior
blacknesses let mine run out in
 the sunny roads Let them be
  released by modulations
   of point by bend of
    line too tiny for
    planning out back
     in hopeful dark
      times or places
      How to hold on
       to a part flat
       or wide enough
        to grasp was
        not too hard
        formerly and
          patterned
          edges cut
          themselves
        What midget
        forms shall
           fall in
           line or
          row beyond
          this wall
          of self A
          key can
        open a car
        Why not me
         O let me
           get in
```

V

SONNET

Matte brandy bottle, adjacent voices, skin
of flank, hip, and ribs trade warmth. You stroke
me, stroke into me. We come together,
come, come back, front on front, where we were.
Ordinary lamplit lovers, we smoke
and whisper. You burn in my cup of oil
and I glow. Our voices flicker, still
alight. As it happens, this never happened.
We sat, traffic-jammed in the rented car
after hours piled up. We were tentative.
You would go again. A barred signal, "love"
hung between us where we stalled. Desire
tautens parallel perpendiculars;
a thin wire lights and shadows where I live.

LATE AFTERNOON

Tired, we drive
through sluggish winter void.
Beneath the steady scansion of the wheels
edgeless roads follow fields
to infinite half-light.

Vast, past hours clot
the space between us.
Each tuft of reed holds,
like a prelude,
echoes of solitude.

You take my hand. Palms press. Fingers
interlock, as if praying for mercy
like the builders of dikes and wharves
beyond Les Saintes-Maries
already behind us.

Through the windshield, grey
with dust and dead insects,
night appraises the ending day,
traces a graph of colors, shadows, shapes
spelling *last time*, nothing more.

We cannot reclaim
the ancient trails of the Camargue we walked on,
nor the lookout posts, cabins and custom house
the inconstant Rhone lost
to the legislation of the sea.

Our evening is like this:
we have anticipated
that our lanes will separate.
Before light withdraws we would like to say
unforgettable words.

JUMP CABLING

When our cars	touched,
When you lifted the hood	of mine
To see the intimate workings	underneath,
When we were bound	together
By a pulse of pure	energy,
When my car like the	princess
In the tale woke with a	start,

I thought why not ride the rest of the way together?

Joseph Bruchac

A MEETING AT THE CROSSROADS

Round the corner I see, ahead of me in the
midst of the crossroads, two cars nose to
nose. Like lovers swapping spit, electricity
shoots from one to another. A Ford and a Chevy,
heedless of miscegenation, they keep nuzzling
up bumper to bumper, while a skinny man in a dark
T-shirt, their procurer, scurries back and forth
to keep the current running, pleading with the
motor to turn over.

Neither one has had enough, though. The generator
whines, but the engine doesn't turn over. Maybe
they'll be there all morning, metal elephants
making slow love. As I go past them I can see
the tail light of the Chevy blinking on and off
in ecstacy.

DON'T ANYBODY MOVE

Who stole my Cadillac, my coupe de ville?
I parked it here five minutes ago.
And who got away with my girl?

Blond curls, eyes of razor-blue,
nine lives to live and none for you.
Who stole my Cadillac, my coupe de ville?

My pomegranate-red custom coupe de ville,
the only one I had in all the world.
And who got away with my girl?

Got my ruby ring and sharkskin suit,
mink necktie and alligator boot,
but who stole my Cadillac, my coupe de ville?

Was it the preacher with his beard of dust,
the sheriff, the banker, somebody I trust
who got away with my girl?

She can't drive, she told me so.
Don't anybody move until I know
who stole my Cadillac, my coupe de ville,
and who got away with my girl.

MARRIED THREE MONTHS

Walter always
took his
bath

first

then sat
in the car

and honked
while Grace bathed

until the day

Grace ran
a dripping wet
nude

to the car

MARRIAGE

Marriage is like that, you know—
two fine folks seated comfortably
in their used Ford motor car
sinking calmly into the sea for years
knowing how they will rise again
separately through water.

THE TROUBLE WITH TRUCK DRIVERS

They're *in front of* me when I start uphill,
clumsy and vulnerable as moths.
Behind when I go down:

They rage and steam after me like big game hunters,
grinding gearshifts into my landscape.

They bring out the worst in me. I follow them
in an empty trance, all spread and self-destructive.

Then I step on the gas,
pass three together on the Turnpike,
leer at them: beep-beep.
They lean on me with their headlights.

Soon the road fades into a stupor of Milky Way wrappers,
radio tunes.

The head drifts over tin fences into pastures
Here's the land and what it does:
blue wildflowers, queen anne's lace, white daisies.

Trucks fly past me, dropping their diesel smell
in the window.

Then here I go again: my foot driven
into the floorboard, past everything.

A crude vengeance on the road, a leveller,
a trader bringing goods, a cow, a horse,
a bale of hay.

I'm getting around another of these bastards,
staring him down, heading for the Howard Johnson's
and the man I fall on at the end of this journey

as if he were a truckdriver, tree climber,
railroad mender, dealer in hard love.

VACATION TRIP

The loudest sound in our car
was Mother being glum:

    Little chiding valves
    a surge of detergent oil
    all that deep chaos
    the relentless accurate fire
    the drive shaft wild to arrive

And tugging along behind in its great big
balloon,
that looming piece of her mind:

"I wish I hadn't come."

THE TRIP

Father and Stevie in the front seat,
Mother and Martha in the back with Grandmother
In a car going West,
Father's vacation of two weeks
Spent on the road,
Lifting the road dust in a cloud
That settles slowly as they pass.

In a town like Santa Fe
They visit the oldest house on the Continent,
Damp as a cellar, with cracked clay walls.
The children whine for ice cream.
Mother buys a postcard for a friend.
Waiting outside, Grandmother looks at the sky
And frowns. It's going to rain.

"Remember what you've seen, Children,"
Father says; "your friends will be interested.
One day you'll have your own children.
When they ask for stories
You can tell them about this."
Then he calls them to the car and drives on,
Hoping that the woman he loved years back
Was right when she told him to see the world.

Behind the motel, the children,
Excited by the early dark,
Scatter with other children on the field,
Boys chasing girls,
Girls outrunning them, shrieking
In the joy of escape, or slowing down,
All delighted by the power of their legs,
Wind on their faces, their hair.

No future tourists can be spotted here,
No writers married to their chairs,
No druggists locking their drugstores at dark,
Walking home, hunched over, in the rain.

EVERYBODY EATS TOO MUCH ANYHOW

You gulp your breakfast and glance at the clock,
Through eleventh hour packing you gallop amok,
You bundle your bags in the back of the car,
You enter, she enters, and there you are.
You clutch the wheel, she clutches the maps,
And longs for a couple of extra laps.
It's *au revoir* to your modest abode,
You're gipsies, away on the open road;
Into the highway you burst like a comet or
Heat waves climbing a Kansas thermometer.
The conversation is sweet as clover,
With breakfast practically hardly over.
"Darling, light me a cigarette?"
"At once and with all my heart, my pet;
And by the way, we are off the track;
We should have turned left a half-mile back."
You swing around with a cheery smile,
Thus far, a mile is only a mile.
The road is romance, so let it wind,
With breakfast an hour or so behind.
Under the tires the pebbles crunch,
And through the dust creep thoughts of lunch.
The speedometer sits on a steady fifty
And more and more does lunch seem nifty.
Your eyes to the road ahead are glued,
she glances about in search of food.
She sees a place. She would like to try it.
She says so. Well, you're already by it.
Ignoring the road, you spot an eatery;
The look of it makes her interior teetery.
She sees a beauty. You're past it again.
Her eyebrows look like ten past ten;
She's simmering now, and so are you,
And *your* brows register ten to two.
She snubs the excuse as you begin it—
That there'll be another one any minute—
She says there won't. It must be a plot;
She's absolutely correct. There's not.

99

You finally find one. You stop and alight.
You're both too annoyed to eat a bite.
Oh, this is the gist of my gipsy song:
Next time carry your lunch along.

A NATURAL HISTORY OF DRAGONS AND UNICORNS MY DAUGHTER AND I HAVE KNOWN

(Written on the Occasion of Her 12th Birthday)

Already we are both fans of the green and golden dragon
   who tumbles gloriously out of the terrible heavens
      not only in books and dreams

for us: He cascades also down the sides of the seagreen '61
   Valiant we painted once together by the ocean,
      trying to outrace the setting Mendocino sun

four years ago with mist rolling in, and he tumbles
   as well down the side of that van which resembles
      nothing so much as a forest dwarf's hutch on wheels

where he silently roars a great bouquet of flowers,
   while his green and scaley winding tail anchors
      round the side window. Rose-white, a Unicorn

edged in icy blue rears opposite our flower-breathing
   fire-eater now, its jewelous horn shining
      by moonlight and headlight, glowing

with a proud shy promise of goodness pure as silver.
   We cannot always be together,
      you and I, and I would have you remember

our fabulous creatures always—the bold Dragon
   as terrible as the horned horse is wonderful, twins of a wisdom
      older by far than we are in our kingdom

of daily things. Here, then, as a reminder, is the image
   of our Unicorn seen silver as he wades into waters ageless
      as the blue sky they reflect, hooves half tangled

in the world's common grasses. Keep him with you
    where you go and try from time to time gazing through
        your eyes as he gazes through his: A sky beating slowly blue

    as the heart of all the air, grass burning green as an emerald's coolly imperial
        and incessant stare, the inner brilliance of all that is natural
            held in that eye of his, which is every bit as real as he is invisible.

DENTYNE

My father always kept
Dentyne in his back pockets
with keys and change
matches and old wrappers.
In the car he sat on it
lifted his ass a little off the seat
slid his stomach into the steering wheel
to reach me a piece. Unwrapping
at stop lights
we chewed together.
There was never much time
without brothers or sisters
days when I got the front seat to myself
to chew with my father
singing with the radio.

DREAM OF A FATHER

Last night, for the first time,
I dreamed of you. Though still tall,
you had at last grown old
your feet failing to grip ground
a cane in one hand, the other
resting hard upon the hood
of that black Pontiac—
the one Mother and I drove
over corrugated roads
filling its vases
with wild flowers.

Once as I lay tantrum-strewn
on the back seat, she cried,
"I cannot stand it any more."
What? Life? Me—a poor
exchange for you?

In this dream (like a snapshot
gradually set in motion)
you moved slowly toward the door
I held open. You said,
"Well, let's go." Where?
You did not tell me.
I awoke before you got in.

MINUET IN A MINOR KEY

Almost touching, almost joining, two
cars come together in a slow
dance beside a roadside inn. No one

watches as a woman in blue transfers
a young boy like a blown-glass
vase from the rusted yellow Mustang

into a vermilion Pinto driven by
a bearded and impatient man. The sun
slips from the sky, a burning city

stealing color from the clustering bodies,
turning them into vapors. Both cars
flee the dark in opposing trajectories

the way fireflies on a summer night
evade the small hands and the collecting jar.
Two evenings later a reunion is witnessed

by the same stucco structure with its
mournful orange roof; the boy is changed
from red to yellow, as if a magician's

wand had control of his spectrum.
Engines spin once more, the speeding
cars recede in opposite directions,

taking no notice of posted limits or
signs of treacherous soft shoulders,
frost heaves ahead.

Patricia Garfinkel

BLIZZARD

We steer our voices through the blizzard.
Mist climbs the car windows. Space collapses
to a green sedan. The birds watch from hidden

perches, cradling small warmth in tightened
feathers, leaning in on fragile bones.
The drift of other winters rises

to hold us to the road: my mother
calling through bay window sunsets to race
the moon home, her fingers etched like winter

branches on the frosted panes. The wind
mounds this road with snow, cups wild
berries in wet flakes, thickens pine

needles with white crayon. Bird cries frenzy
the air. Our voices join the birds who wait for
our eyes to freeze like berries in the face of winter.

THE DRAGON OF RED LIGHTS

The dragon of red lights
Eats the highway.
Ascending or descending the black
Pennsylvania mountains,
Over the depths of rock.
No blame.

The days follow upon one another,
Like cards in the deck:
The Fool, the Knight of Cups,
The Magician.

We talk about what divides

Us, what binds.
The cards fluttered like
The flat hands of the yellow aspen
In the moonlight.

Yesterday's palmreader said she
Danced in gypsy camps
When she was younger,
Felt the sting.
My love line crosses
Your fate
Line. You bleed.

We don't mention the
Little ghost
Lingering on the side of the road,
Sometimes a possum upturned,
Sometimes a boy's dog spilling red meat.
Sometimes a glitter of broken glass
As we pass by at
Sixty,
Thirty years from the end.

The days follow,
One on another,
Like the things we give each other:
A ring, a word,
Some space in the light.

VI

AUTO WRECK

Its quick soft silver bell beating, beating,
And down the dark one ruby flare
Pulsing out red light like an artery,
The ambulance at top speed floating down
Past beacons and illuminated clocks
Wings in a heavy curve, dips down,
And brakes speed, entering the crowd.
The doors leap open, emptying light;
Stretchers are laid out, the mangled lifted
And stowed into the little hospital.
Then the bell, breaking the hush, tolls once,
And the ambulance with its terrible cargo
Rocking, slightly rocking, moves away,
As the doors, an afterthought, are closed.

We are deranged, walking among the cops
Who sweep glass and are large and composed.
One is still making notes under the light.
One with a bucket douches ponds of blood
Into the street and gutter.
One hangs lanterns on the wrecks that cling,
Empty husks of locusts, to iron poles.

Our throats were tight as tourniquets,
Our feet were bound with splints, but now,
Like convalescents intimate and gauche,
We speak through sickly smiles and warn
With the stubborn saw of common sense,
The grim joke and the banal resolution.
The traffic moves around with care,
But we remain, touching a wound
That opens to our richest horror.
Already old, the question Who shall die?
Becomes unspoken Who is innocent?

For death in war is done by hands;
Suicide has cause and stillbirth, logic;
And cancer, simple as a flower, blooms.
But this invites the occult mind,
Cancels our physics with a sneer,
And spatters all we knew of denouement
Across the expedient and wicked stones.

BIG CRASH OUT WEST

They call streets "boulevards" and build them huge
Where grandpa's ox-cart could not budge;
Here's room for elbows, land of the brave fourth gears.
Speed is the bridge for spanning loneliness.
Until.
           This is the western way to die.
And when the car stops burning, thar he'll lie,
Surrounded by the brothers of his lodge.
O crash for whom their boredoms cry,
Is there—in your sensuous instant—time to guess
At what's unspent, unsensuous years
Never hot with doubt nor faith nor reverence for tears?

WRECK

Damn fool feeling her up
with both hands and one or more feet
pulled beside me at the light
—ice-blue Ford with a fire inside—
looked at me once and winked, then
left screaming, rubber smoking on a February street
behind him in a swath as wide
as jubilation. It was quick:
two can die
so fast; two blocks contain a life.
Outrageously they burned away from stop
and could not stop again except to meet
outrageous luck
in the face of a truck.

I saw the flame flare out,
I saw the chrome curled melting back
on flesh, and steel burnt crisply black,
burning hand on burning thigh
and panic frozen into burning eyes;
                    and

I have seen it since I have have seen
meat on braziers grin and wink
and melt to ash. I have seen
fire freeze and ice burn
and bloody smoke blown upwind
into visions. I have seen
them die—
and waked,
cursing Ford and fire and two too dead
to cool the conflagration in my head.

ANOTHER KIND OF BURNING

The south wind's molded by a spine of hill—
tree-dense, Appalachian—that from miles of woods
brings the scent of another kind of burning,
the fume of life, hair-thin, wrist-thick,
that last season's and the one before's and before that's
leaves resurrect,

and all the creeks composed of decomposings
comb the hillsides, shape roads. Three meet
where Back Creek crosses under a low
highway bridge. Among those who died here
was a boy

already caught by the same Heraclitean flux:
a father at sixteen in his mother-in-law's house,
driven out by women, driving too fast,
met at this crossroads
by the triple goddess.

The tracks of burning on the macadam's
what's left—that and
the wrist-thin, unbroken neck
of an infant now fatherless
in fact.

MORNING RUSH

The undersides of leaves smack
the bright early light around;
frost does the same, and chrome
makes many mirrors moving by
on hordes of chariots.

Gun that motor.
Hold onto your hat. You are one
of many going past faster
than the ground would have you do
as it lies patient, pummelled,
planning a long revenge.

Grackles and sparrows fall from the trees.
Crows drop to dissect
last night's smashed rabbit
or possum, who moved blind
across the highway in the endless trip
between food and home, taking survival
seriously

and never going fast enough.

HIGHWAY: MICHIGAN

Here from the field's edge we survey
The progress of the jaded. Mile
On mile of traffic from the town
Rides by, for at the end of day
The time of workers is their own.

They jockey for position on
The strip reserved for passing only.
The drivers from production lines
Hold to advantage dearly won.
They toy with death and traffic fines.

Acceleration is their need:
A mania keeps them on the move
Until the toughest nerves are frayed.
They are the prisoners of speed
Who flee in what their hands have made.

The pavement smokes when two cars meet
And steel rips through conflicting steel.
We shiver at the siren's blast.
One driver, pinned beneath the seat,
Escapes from the machine at last.

A RACCOON

lies broken

on the broken line of a road. Like
the car that killed it, I speed by.

My eye has sighted the plight in
the small and pointed face, and
blinked

at the pink entrails that trail
from its belly. But it is the paw
that makes my mind stare.

What is there that makes the paw
reach up? and the five fingers
at the end of the reach, bend

like a hand? They say that animals
are our innocence, what we were before
Eden, and the Fall.

Though I cannot understand it all
I stay on my side of the broken line
that divides the going from the coming.

TRAVELING THROUGH THE DARK

Traveling through the dark I found a deer
dead on the edge of the Wilson River road.
It is usually best to roll them into the canyon:
that road is narrow; to swerve might make more dead.

By glow of the tail-light I stumbled back of the car
and stood by the heap, a doe, a recent killing;
she had stiffened already, almost cold.
I dragged her off; she was large in the belly.

My fingers touching her side brought me the reason—
her side was warm; her fawn lay there waiting,
alive, still, never to be born.
Beside that mountain road I hesitated.

The car aimed ahead its lowered parking lights;
under the hood purred the steady engine.
I stood in the glare of the warm exhaust turning red;
around our group I could hear the wilderness listen.

I thought hard for us all—my only swerving—
then pushed her over the edge into the river.

Sarah Cotterill

CUTTING REDBUD: AN ACCIDENTAL DEATH

> *"I gathered up the leaves*
> *and gave them back."*
>> The Purgatorio

The wound spreads to the ground.
You are amazed and let the axe fall;
the leaves go on bleeding and your limb

now, a mystery, joins them.
Leaf spines arch and snap
under your hands, woman,

you leaning.
The ground pine seems to stand
and the standing pine violently

to lie down.
Then things are
as they are, and dropping

the redbud, you dream toward
the car. It starts and moves, running with your
blood, racing it, the flow of

concrete, the sprung visual field.
Something is in the way, then not—
the wheel keeps folding and loosening

the car keeps heeling

over.
In sleep I fell the redbud leaves
thinking, at least to have them.
                              You scream.
I gather up the leaves and give them back.

AMERICAN CLASSIC

It's a classic American scene—
a car stopped off the road
and a man trying to repair it.

The woman who stays in the car
in the classic American scene
stares back at the freeway traffic.

They look surprised, and ashamed
to be so helpless . . .
let down in the middle of the road!

To think that their car would do this!
They look like mountain people
whose son has gone against the law.

But every night they set out food
and the robber goes skulking back to the trees.
That's how it is with the car . . .

it's theirs, they're stuck with it.
Now they know what it's like to sit
and see the world go whizzing by.

In the fume of carbon monoxide and dust
they are not such good Americans
as they thought they were.

The feeling of being left out
through no fault of your own, is common.
That's why I say, an American classic.

Michael West

PARTS MAN

At the last rush of summer
he turns up his palms and face
to the cool October rains
gathering on his lips
in the first syllables of death.

Endlessly shifting
the wide black catalogue,
ordering the random intenstines of cars—
each spiral landed worm and
shackled leaf, sandcasted pinion
and spider. These appear
indestructible, so hard so precise.
But they come back always
bleeding their fine rust
given up for exchange.

Expecting nothing of autumn
he finally receives it, even steel
gives up to the rain.
And passengers in long sedans
hear all the wheels
hiss in the street, turning
anxiously into themselves.

THOREAU

It is when I work on the old Volvo,
lying on my back among the sockets,
wrenches, nuts, and bolts,
with the asphalt grinding the skin
over my shoulderblades, and with the cold grease
dripping onto my eyeglasses,
that I think of Thoreau
on his morning walks around the pond
dreaming of self-sufficiency.
I think of the odometer that shows
eight circuits of the planet.
I drop the transmission and loosen
the bolts around the bellhousing.
I take it in both hands, jerk,
and it pops like a sliced melon.
Carefully, so I won't damage
the diaphragm, I remove the clutch
and place it on a clean cloth
beside the jackstand. I look
at the illustrations in the manual,
and I think of the lists that Thoreau made.
By the time I get to the flywheel,
grease is clotted in my hair,
my knuckles are raw and bleeding
against the crankcase, and I am thinking
of civil disobedience. I am looking
up into the dark heaven of machinery,
the constellations of flaking gaskets,
and I am thinking of Thoreau's dry cow,
of his cornstalks splintered by hail.

EVERY SATURDAY HE STANDS

Saturdays he stands on his bike
seat, grips the lip of the leaning
hubcap hanging fence, and sees
the world's worst accident: fender
to fender cars tilt to their shadows,
wheels sucked into weeds are still.

Now he knows: metal bleeds
and all bodies fall off edges
into this field, quiver,
and die in the darkness of oil.

Yet, this dark is a magnet, gears pull,
and so his hubcap face over the fence
reflects the mystery of metal:
a craftsman could make these cars
sit straight, with art and love this epic
could again move, and he knows grease
will fit his hands like tight, sheer gloves—

intent on rusty stains,
he does not hear distant sirens
nor see his smile distort
in the hundred hanging moons.

1948 PLYMOUTH ABANDONED ON THE ICE

The crunch of the salvage yard
would have been easy: this death
is too gradual, the whisper of
gasoline evaporating.

Who left it here
in the middle of the lake
this late in winter?
It waits on a shrinking pupil,
tires carving slow ruts
as though spinning in white sand.

Children sit on shore, pitch rocks
through its side windows,
hold their breaths.
Old men make bets on which morning
they'll glance out their cabins,
see it has fallen through to the

other world.
The hoist of water lowers
it gently, tires
down. The lake bottom
is a hundred thousand miles
from dry asphalt.

Inside the windshield,
one last sphere of air still
nudges a silvery balloon that will not deflate,
a loyal eye that stares
for years at the speedometer
waiting for it to turn over.

David McElroy

ODE TO A DEAD DODGE

Now corn pushes past the foam
rubber front seat where it sprouted,
pale and aiming like a drunk for the light
up front where glass and guessing
became concrete. One ear taps
code on a dud horn.

The corn drives on, gunning 'til fall
the engine, which, as it now stands,
is a sumac, V crotch in the stem,
four-barrelled leaves doing the job
while all around hang those red fuzzy
berries. Very good, I've heard, for tea.

ABANDONING YOUR CAR IN A SNOWSTORM:
ROSSLYN, VIRGINIA

It is better
than leaving your wife or your nagging lover
could ever be.

It is better than anything
you have ever bought, better
than the best nights of sex in your life,
even better than quitting your job.

As you open your door to reclaim your feet
from the hungry clutch, you know
you are on to something: You are suddenly
a drowning man whose last stride has found
the ocean floor, a vagabond with a roof
over his head for the first time.

Around you, mothers curse red lights,
men in wide ties are reduced to a hilarious impotence.
All the revving in the world will not move them,
all their stalled money cannot buy rain.

And there you are,
Toyota-less and dancing to the Cadillac pace
of sure movement, Johnny Travolta Fred Astaire
by God the world is beautiful and glass-less
and the Shah of Iran too is stalled in some Siberia
with his billions and his quiet wife, and all the oil
wells in the world will not lead him from his private Rosslyn.

If you go anywhere, dear Shah,
you must learn to trust your feet again,
I call to him from my clean and snow-swept escalator
to the nation's capital, and move on—

a ribbon whirling between the stalled cars
on these beautiful bridges,
calling *Goodbye Exxon*
Goodbye gas-line anti-freeze

Goodbye you ugly Detroit.

KLAXON

All day cars mooed and shrieked,
Hollered and bellowed and wept
Upon the road.
They slid by with bits of fur attached,
Fox-tails and rabbit-legs,
The skulls and horns of deer,
Cars with yellow spectacles
Or motorcycle monocle,
Cars whose gold eyes burnt
With a too-rich battery,
Murderous cars and manslaughter cars,
Chariots from whose foreheads leapt
Silver women of ardent bosom.
Ownerless, passengerless, driverless,
They came to anyone
And with headlights full of tears
Begged for a master,
For someone to drive them
For the familiar chauffeur.
Limousines covered with pink slime
Of children's blood
Turned into the open fields
And fell over into ditches,
The wheels kicking helplessly.
Taxis begged trees to step inside,
Automobiles begged of posts
The whereabouts of their mother.
But no one wished to own them any more,
Everyone wished to walk.

Charles Vandersee

THE EXACT SAME PLACES

Old songs of the island Albion
make up a set in dreams,
dreams in which Greek pots perform adequately
their stereotyped routines.

We sit through the whole set
scratching our necks with curtain rods,
with dishtowels wipe the dust off hooves,
and applaud, being polite.

But get the crockery off the stage
and let the cars perform,
the versatiles! The way
to hear best is move around.

The highway songs take us in a rush
to where the poets used to,
riding nightingales and winds:
those places, almost the exact same places.

Acknowledgments

Deirdra Baldwin: "Remembering the Automobile" from INSIDE OUTSIDE by Deirdra Baldwin, with drawings by Gene Davis. Copyright © 1982 by Poets and Artists Collaborative. Reprinted by permission of the author.

David Barker: "Packard" first appeared in *Goldermood Rainbow*, 1981. Reprinted by permission of Goldermood Rainbow Press.

Gerald Barrax: "Slow Drivers" from THE DEATHS OF ANIMALS AND LESSER GODS by Gerald Barrax © 1985 Callaloo Press. Reprinted by permission of Callaloo Press.

Marvin Bell: "Who's in Charge Here?" from SEGUES: A CORRESPONDENCE IN POETRY by William Stafford and Marvin Bell. Copyright © 1983 by William Stafford and Marvin Bell. First appeared in *The American Poetry Review*. Reprinted by permission of David R. Godine, Publisher, Boston.

Elizabeth Bishop: "Filling Station" from THE COMPLETE POEMS 1927-1979 by Elizabeth Bishop. Copyright © 1955, 1969 by Elizabeth Bishop. Reprinted by permission of Farrar, Straus and Giroux, Inc.

John Peale Bishop: "This Dim and Ptolemaic Man," (Copyright 1933, John Peale Bishop; copyright renewed) in THE COLLECTED POEMS OF JOHN PEALE BISHOP, Ed. Allen Tate. Copyright 1948, 1976 Charles Scribner's Sons. Reprinted with the permission of Charles Scribner's Sons.

Michael Blumenthal: "Abandoning Your Car in a Snowstorm" from SYMPATHETIC MAGIC by Michael Blumenthal, published by Water Mark Press, © 1980 by Michael Blumenthal. First printed in *The Washingtonian*. Reprinted by permission of the author.

Robert Bly: "Come with Me" from THE LIGHT AROUND THE BODY: *Poems* by Robert Bly. Copyright © 1964 by Robert Bly. Reprinted by permission of Harper & Row, Publishers, Inc.

Terry Borst: "Random Wheels" is printed by permission of the author.

David Bottoms: "In the Black Camaro" from IN A U-HAUL NORTH OF DAMASCUS (1983) by David Bottoms. Copyright © 1982 by David Bottoms. By permission of William Morrow & Company. First appeared in *Poetry*, June, 1982.

Joseph Bruchac: "A Meeting at the Crossroads" is printed by permission of the author.

Michael Casey: "Driving while under the influence" appeared in *Harvard Magazine*. Reprinted by permission of the author.

Siv Cedering: "A Raccoon" is printed by permission of the author.

Amy Clampitt: Agreeable Monsters" first appeared in *Antaeus*, No. 33, Spring, 1979. Reprinted by permission of the author.

Constance Clark: "Morning Rush" is printed by permission of the author.

Shirley Cochrane: "Dream of a Father" is printed by permission of the author.

Gregory Corso: "Poets Hitch-hiking on the Highway" from THE HAPPY BIRTHDAY OF DEATH. Copyright © 1960 by New Directions Publishing Corporation. Reprinted by permission of the publisher.

Sarah Cotterill: "Cutting Redbud: An Accidental Death" from THE HIVE BURNING, published by The Sleeping Bird Press. Copyright © 1983 by Sarah Cotterill. First appeared in *The Webster Review*. Reprinted by permission of the author.

870886

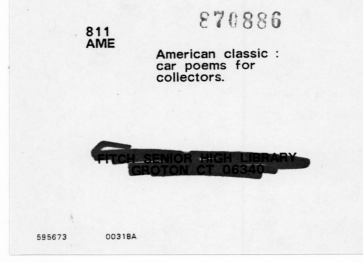

Typeset by Dan Johnson in Garth type at The Writer's Center, Bethesda, MD.
Printed by Smith Lithograph Corporation, Rockville, MD.